DECADES OF THE 20th CENTURY

IN COLOR

THE 1950s

FROM THE KOREAN WAR TO ELVIS **REVISED EDITION**

STEPHEN FEINSTEIN

Library of Congress Cataloging-in-Publication Data

Feinstein, Stephen.
  The 1950s from the Korean War to Elvis / Stephen Feinstein.— Rev. ed.
    p. cm. — (Decades of the 20th century in color)
  Includes index.
  ISBN 0-7660-2635-3
    1. United States—Civilization—1945– —Juvenile literature.
  2. Nineteen fifties—Juvenile literature. I. Title. II. Series: Feinstein, Stephen. Decades of the 20th century in color.
  E169.12.F447 2006
  973.92—dc22

                                    2005019868

Printed in the United States of America

10 9 8 7 6 5 4 3 2 1

Illustration Credits: AP/ Wide World Photos, pp. 4, 9, 10, 16, 17, 19, 20, 22, 23, 26, 28, 29, 30, 39, 41, 43, 46, 49, 50, 54, 57, 58; Dwight D. Eisenhower Library, p. 34; Enslow Publishers, Inc., pp. 6, 55; Everett Collection, Inc., pp. 18, 21, 24; JoAnne Olian, ed., *Everyday Fashions of the Forties, As Pictured in Sears Catalogs* (New York: Dover Publications, Inc., 1992), pp. 11, 12; March of Dimes, p. 56; National Aeronautics and Space Administration (NASA), p. 53; Library of Congress, pp. 13, 14, 25, 31, 32, 45, 47; National Archives, pp. 35, 37, 38, 40; Unisys Corporation, p. 52; Wham-O Inc., p. 15.

All interior collages composed by Enslow Publishers, Inc. Images used are courtesy of the previously credited rights holders, above.

Cover Illustrations: AP/ Wide World Photos; Everett Collection, Inc.; The New York Public Library.

Every effort has been made to locate the copyright owners of the pictures used in this book. If due acknowledgment has not been made, we sincerely regret the omission.

Enslow Publishers, Inc.
40 Industrial Road
Box 398
Berkeley Heights, NJ 07922
USA

http://www.enslow.com

Contents

The 1950s were seriously affected by the scientific advances of the previous decade, especially the atomic bomb. After the United States used the atomic bomb (above) in Japan to end World War II, the Cold War began. The Soviet Union was racing to build weapons as dangerous as those of the United States. As a result, Americans of the 1950s often lived in fear of the possibility of nuclear war.

Introduction

The decade of the 1950s was a time of great change in American life. In 1945, a victorious United States had emerged from World War II as the wealthiest, most powerful nation on Earth. America entered a period of growth and prosperity that would last throughout the 1950s. Jobs were plentiful. More Americans could realize the American dream—a home of their own, perhaps in one of the new suburbs springing up all over the country.

On the one hand, life was good. Americans had many happy hours of family togetherness, either on family vacations or at home, huddled around their television sets. On the other hand, something was very wrong. Americans' fear of the Soviet Union and communism resulted in family fallout shelters, Senator Joseph McCarthy's campaign of intimidation against those he accused of having Communist "sympathies," the Korean War, and the building of a huge nuclear arsenal. The 1950s would go down in history as a decade of sharp contrasts and unique happenings.

People drove everywhere in the 1950s —to the suburban shopping malls, to their jobs, to drive-in fast-food stands, to drive-in movies, to visit friends and relatives, to explore the next state, or to visit the nation's fabulous parklands. Often they drove just for the sake of driving.

The American Dream

In contrast to the years of economic hardship during the Great Depression of the 1930s and the strict rationing of goods during the years of World War II, the 1950s were a time of consumerism. A consumer-oriented lifestyle was developing among the rapidly growing middle class. All sorts of things were now available to Americans. Many people now had money to spend on television sets and household appliances such as refrigerators, dishwashers, and washing machines. Americans by the millions also bought cars. And the ultmate goal of the American dream—home ownership—was now also within reach of a great many Americans.

To make it easier and more convenient for American consumers to spend their money, some businesses during the 1950s began offering credit cards. Diner's Club provided the first credit card. Diner's Club was formed by Frank X. McNamara, an attorney. One day, in 1950, McNamara was embarrassed when he found himself short of cash after eating dinner in a restaurant. The Diner's Club credit card allowed club members to dine at twenty-seven New York City restaurants. Instead of having to carry cash around, Diner's Club members only had to show a Diner's Club credit card. American Express began issuing credit cards in 1958. More than 250,000 Americans eagerly signed up for the credit cards during one three-month period. Bank of America then jumped on the bandwagon, issuing BankAmericards (which later became Visa). Today's MasterCard grew out of credit cards issued by banks in Chicago and California.

Americans and Their Automobiles

In a television commercial, Dinah Shore sang, "See the U.S.A. in Your Chevrolet." And Americans set out to do just that. General Motors' Chevrolet was one of the most popular cars during the 1950s. By the end of the decade, there were no fewer than forty-six different Chevrolet models available.

Automobile manufacturers sent a loud and clear message to Americans: Cars are fun—and it is fun to drive! Americans heard the message and bought far more cars than in any previous period. Especially popular were big, long cars with tail fins.

By 1952, there were already more than 52 million cars on the roads across America. Traffic congestion was becoming a problem. There simply were not enough roads to handle the increasing amount of traffic. So in 1956, Congress passed the National Defense Highway Act, in part to be able to move armed forces quickly around the country if necessary. The law would build a nationwide system of interstate freeways. The planned 42,500 miles of divided highway, which took decades to complete, would eventually link every major city in the country.

The Suburbs

In the 1950s, those who had achieved the ultimate goal of the American dream were living in the best of all possible

An aerial view of the suburban development of Levittown, Long Island (below), in 1950. All of the 17,447 homes looked pretty much the same. People who lived there developed a sense of community.

Actor Gregory Peck in a scene from the 1955 film, *The Man in the Gray Flannel Suit*. Gray flannel suits were considered the appropriate "uniform" for the American businessman in the 1950s.

worlds—the American suburbs. At least, that is how it must have seemed to those who had yet to attain this goal. Suburban middle-class American family life was glowingly portrayed each night on television as the epitome of easy living.

The Man in the Gray Flannel Suit

The new American suburban lifestyle was characterized by conformity in external appearances as well as in personal goals, opinions, and values. Not only did the streets and houses look the same, but so did the styles of clothing. The typical suburban employee of a big corporation, who came to be called an "organization man," commuted to work in the city. He wore a gray flannel suit or some equally conservative "uniform" to work. He kept his hair short. He usually wore a narrow-brimmed hat while traveling to and from work.

The organization man's job was important to him—whether he liked his work or not. He liked the suburban lifestyle it let him lead.

Black Turtlenecks and Beatniks

Some suburbanites eventually rejected what they considered the hollow values of the suburbs and the corporate world. Others were also turned off by the growing conformity they believed would stifle creativity in American life. Known as Beatniks, these people—among them writer Jack Kerouac and poet Allen Ginsberg—rejected the culture of materialism and the conformity of organization men. They valued experience more than things, spontaneity more than routine. They challenged commonly held notions about how people should live, work, and play. Jack Kerouac set out on the road, crisscrossing America many times and even traveling through Mexico, in search of adventure and freedom. His 1957 novel, *On the Road*, is a fictional account of his experiences.

The Beat lifestyle typically involved sexual freedom and the use of drugs such as marijuana and alcohol. The Beatniks could be seen hanging out in coffeehouses. They listened to jazz music and Beat poetry. Of course, not one of them would be wearing gray flannel—or any other kind of suit. Many of the men, however, wore a different uniform: black turtleneck sweaters, blue jeans, and sandals. Beatnik women typically wore black leotards and short skirts. Apparently, even those who rejected corporate ideas were not immune to conformity of some sort.

"Truly Feminine Women"

Throughout the 1950s, women were often portrayed in magazines and advertisements as domestic servants whose main duty was catering to the needs of their husbands and children. According to *Life* magazine, a "truly feminine" woman's proper place was in the home, especially the kitchen.

In real life, however, more women were beginning to work outside the home in the 1950s. They had little time to prepare elaborate meals. By 1956, 32 percent of all women were part of the American labor force. Unfortunately, most women had to work at low-paying clerical, assembly-line,

Women, like their husbands, wanted to follow a very particular fashion style in the 1950s. Most wore feminine, yet tailored dresses (below), which were convenient for those who continued to work outside the home.

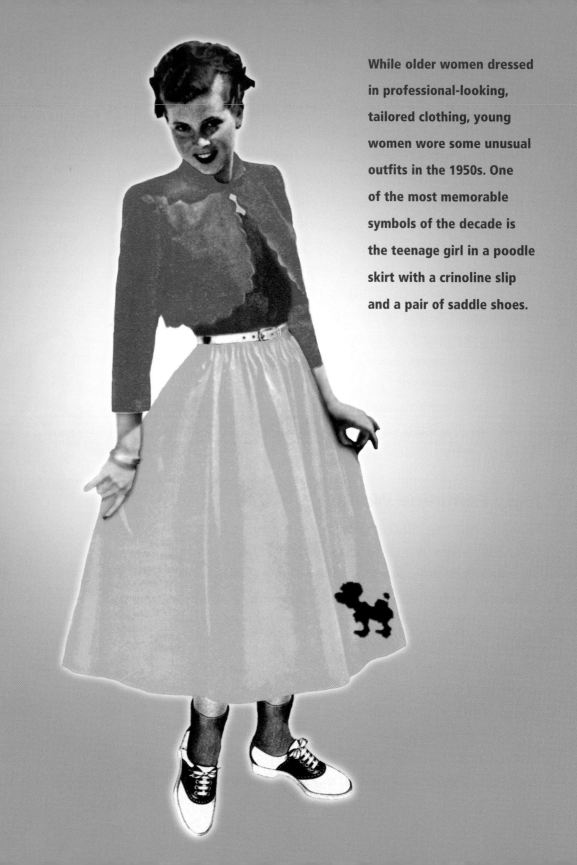

While older women dressed in professional-looking, tailored clothing, young women wore some unusual outfits in the 1950s. One of the most memorable symbols of the decade is the teenage girl in a poodle skirt with a crinoline slip and a pair of saddle shoes.

or service jobs. Only a small number of women held management positions or practiced a profession. When women went into the kitchen after a hard day's work, they were likely to heat up frozen TV dinners for their families.

Although women's roles were changing, the most popular fashions of the 1950s emphasized women's femininity and sexuality. By 1950, Christian Dior's "New Look" had become the height of fashion. Dior's clothing enhanced a woman's natural curves, creating the classic hourglass figure—skintight tailoring around the bosom, a narrow waist, and a full skirt that often flared out. Stiletto heels were popular, and women did not feel completely dressed until they had painted their lips bright red. The well-dressed woman often wore a hat in public. Career women, dressed in suits, always wore gloves.

The Cold War: The Era of Duck and Cover

But there was more going on in the 1950s than interesting fashions. In September 1949, Americans learned that their Cold War adversary, the Soviet Union, had built an atomic bomb. America was no longer the only nation with nuclear weapons. To Americans, the world had suddenly become much more dangerous. Soon, air-raid drills were being conducted across the country. When the siren sounded, people were to go to the nearest air-raid shelter and stay there until they heard the all-clear siren.

During the early years of the Cold War, Americans began to develop a deep-seated fear of communism and the Soviet Union. This 1938 pamphlet (above) shows the fearful attitude with which many Americans regarded the Communist threat. By the 1950s, such attitudes were even more pervasive.

Many Americans were so fearful that a nuclear war could take place at any moment that they erected bomb shelters (above) in their backyards. Stocked with food and supplies, many people believed the bomb shelters could help them survive the many long months or even years of devastation after a nuclear war.

Even schoolchildren participated in air-raid drills. At the sound of the siren, teachers shouted, "Take cover!" The children would immediately follow the "duck-and-cover" routine they had been taught: They would get under their desks and put their head between their knees and their hands over their head. They were warned not to look at the window, because they would be blinded by the flash of the nuclear explosion.

Although Americans were terrified of what could happen to them in a nuclear war, it is doubtful that many took the civil defense drills seriously. People were well aware of the incredible destruction that resulted from an atomic bomb. So when people were told to stay indoors, or to avoid looking at the window, they had good reason to wonder how these measures could save them.

Still, there were many who believed they could survive a nuclear attack if they had access to a bomb shelter. Some Americans bought their own family shelters, which were installed in their backyards. Those who bought fallout shelters believed they were preventing the American dream from turning into the American nightmare.

Popular Fads and Pastimes

Americans in the 1950s were caught up in many popular fads. Perhaps to take their minds off the looming threats to America's security, people were enthusiastic about whatever seemed to be fun. College students could be seen stuffing themselves into telephone booths and cars, as if conducting serious research into the number of people that could fit into a small space. Some people stared in fascination as wire coils called Slinkies walked down flights of stairs. Some played with globs of moldable silicone called Silly Putty. Others tossed Frisbees.

Perhaps the most popular fad of the decade was the Hula-Hoop, first introduced in 1958 by Arthur Melin and Richard Knerr of Wham-O Manufacturing. By 1959, millions of young Americans were swinging Hula-Hoops around their hips, and soon, Hula-Hoop contests were being held all around the country.

The Hula-Hoop (below) was one of the most popular toy fads of the 1950s.

After the great success of movies such as *The Wild One*, starring Marlon Brando (left), it became "cool" to wear a black leather jacket and act tough. Teens who did so became known as "greasers." Some greasers joined youth gangs, which were often seen as a threat to conservative adults.

Young Rebels

In 1955, *Rebel Without a Cause* became a big hit with American teenagers. They identified with the film's young star, James Dean (above), who blamed his parents for his state of confusion and anguish. Many teens in the 1950s, especially those growing up in suburbs, were bored by the blandness of their surroundings. They were confused by society's standards and expectations for them, and resentful of adults' lack of understanding.

Fictional characters showing the concerns of 1950s teenagers appeared in literature as well as in film. Teen readers found their spokesman in Holden Caulfield, the teenage hero of J. D. Salinger's novel *The Catcher in the Rye* (1951). Holden Caulfield shared their frustration with the hypocrisy of adult values.

In 1954, the young actor Marlon Brando starred in *The Wild One.* In the film, he played the leader of a motorcycle gang. The movie inspired young people who identified with the bikers' desire to test the limits of society's tolerance for delinquent behavior. While young people related to the film's heroes, older Americans were becoming concerned with the problems of juvenile delinquency and gang-related crime. Movies such as *The Blackboard Jungle* (1955) pointed out the ugly behavior of unruly youth in New York City's schools.

Despite the sometimes drab conformity Americans of the 1950s showed in fashion and in their choices to live in suburbs, they seemed to enjoy films that depicted far-fetched, fantastic events, as in the 1953 version of *War of the Worlds* (below).

Creatures From Outer Space

As if Americans in the 1950s did not have enough to worry about with nuclear weapons, there was something new to fear—an invasion from outer space! Hollywood produced

a number of science-fiction films dealing with extraterrestrial visitors, such as *War of the Worlds* (1953) and *Invasion of the Body Snatchers* (1956). Many people were either thrilled or horrified by the antics of space creatures on the big screen. Others reported seeing "flying saucers"—strange lights in the night skies over America. Nobody could prove whether the UFOs (unidentified flying objects), as the lights came to be called, were real—perhaps visitors from another planet—or just a figment of people's imagination.

New Ideas in the Movies

Movie producers in the 1950s were afraid that Americans would be so fascinated by television and all the entertainment they could enjoy in their own living rooms, that they would forget to go to the movies. So the movie industry came up with new ideas to attract an audience. They began to use a wide-screen process known as CinemaScope, often presenting biblical spectacles with casts of thousands—films such as *The Ten Commandments* (1956) and *Ben-Hur* (1959).

Producers also made movies that gave the illusion of three dimensions. In 3-D horror films such as *House of Wax* (1953), *It Came from Outer Space* (1953), and *Creature from the Black Lagoon* (1954), the illusion of depth was so vivid that movie-goers would often duck as things seemed to leap off the

The title character of *The Incredible Shrinking Man* (above) finds himself shrinking after exposure to atomic fallout. This 1957 film captured America's growing fears of atomic energy.

screen and into their laps. There was only one catch—in order to experience the third dimension, moviegoers had to wear special glasses. Many people found these glasses annoying. Some even reported getting headaches.

TV Westerns and Millions of Little Cowboys

Along with sitcoms and variety shows, Westerns were among the most popular television shows of the 1950s. Galloping across the screen were popular cowboys such as Hopalong Cassidy, the Lone Ranger, the Cisco Kid, Roy Rogers, and Gene Autry.

Programs such as *The Lone Ranger* (above) appealed to children as well as adults. The popularity of Westerns even caused a fashion trend among young boys, who dressed in cowboy hats and fringed shirts like their favorite television stars.

Westerns especially appealed to children, who spent long hours in front of the television, riding along with their favorite heroes. Before long, millions of young children were prowling the streets of America, wearing big cowboy hats and firing their toy cap guns at each other in mock gunfights. By the mid-1950s, more sophisticated Westerns such as *Gunsmoke* and *Have Gun Will Travel* were being made. These shows became popular mainly with adult audiences.

Comedy Comes to TV

Television was so popular in the 1950s in part because it was still a novelty to most American families. It also provided a form of entertainment that appealed to a broad range of people. It quickly became a main source of family entertainment.

Television sitcoms such as *Leave It to Beaver, Ozzie and Harriet, Father Knows Best,* and *I Love Lucy* (above) presented a world in which everyone lived in harmony. Parents never raised their voices in anger. The happy characters easily solved any minor problem.

Despite her worldwide fame and image as a sex symbol, Marilyn Monroe (right) was not as successful in her personal life. Her marriage to baseball star Joe DiMaggio ended in divorce, as did her marriage to playwright Arthur Miller. In 1962, she died from an overdose of sleeping pills at the age of thirty-six.

Millions of homes throughout America were filled with the sounds of laughter, thanks to wildly popular television comedians such as Lucille Ball, Jackie Gleason, and Milton "Uncle Miltie" Berle, known as Mr. Television.

Marilyn Monroe and the Sexual Revolution

The sexual revolution that would erupt in America in the 1960s was starting to simmer in the 1950s. Perhaps the one person who best symbolized Americans' fantasies and notions about sexuality in the 1950s was Marilyn Monroe. Born Norma Jean Mortenson in 1926, Monroe grew up to become a screen sensation during the 1950s. She starred in such films as *Gentlemen Prefer Blondes* (1953), *How to Marry a Millionaire* (1953), and *Some Like It Hot* (1959). Marilyn Monroe did indeed have a beautiful face and body, but she was also a fine actress and singer, and she put her comedic skills to good use by satirizing the Hollywood sex goddess role that made her famous.

Elvis Presley (below), one of the most popular rock singers, became known as the King of Rock 'n' Roll.

Rock 'n' Roll

In his hit rock 'n' roll song "Roll Over Beethoven," singer Chuck Berry told Beethoven, who symbolized classical music, to "roll over." He might just as well have also advised every other older musical style to "roll over" and get out of the way—because rock 'n' roll was here to stay. Due to its almost instant popularity among America's teens, rock 'n' roll swept aside all other forms of music.

Rock 'n' roll did not just appear overnight. It was based on a combination of black blues and R&B (rhythm and blues), and white blues, or "hillbilly" music. What these kinds of music had in common was their soulful expression of

Dick Clark (above) hosted the successful television program, *American Bandstand*, which showcased the latest songs and musicians. It was also a hit with teenagers because it included lots of dancing. By watching (or participating in) the show, teenagers could learn the newest dance steps.

raw emotion. Rock 'n' roll was a huge success because it had a winning formula—simple melodies, basic chords, and a backbeat. It was loud and sexy. There was nothing subtle about it. And it was great to dance to, as seen on Dick Clark's television show *American Bandstand*. An added benefit of rock 'n' roll was that older Americans, including the parents of teenagers, hated it. When young Americans went crazy over rock 'n' roll, the older generation reacted with alarm, fearing that the music was wildly sexual and would lead young people astray. So millions of American teens, especially those with a rebellious streak, became devoted fans of 1950s rock stars such as Jerry Lee Lewis, Buddy Holly, Chuck Berry, Little Richard, and Fats Domino. The biggest rock 'n' roll sensation was Elvis Presley, who came to be called the King of Rock 'n' Roll.

Rock 'n' roll was able to succeed in part because there were so many young people to enjoy it. A post–World War II baby boom led to such a high birthrate that, by 1958, one third of America's population was under the age of fifteen. This new generation of Americans, who came to be known as baby boomers, would eventually create a new youth culture based on rock 'n' roll music.

Jazz—Some Like It Cool

True jazz fans in the 1950s were not about to give up the music they loved. While rock 'n' roll got hotter, jazz became cool—real cool. In previous decades, jazz had been widely popular, mainly because people liked to dance to it. But by the 1950s, the most interesting and innovative jazz was not dance music, and the audience for it was much smaller. Fans enjoyed listening to the brilliant, intricate improvisations of musicians such as Miles Davis, Theolonious Monk, Dizzy Gillespie, Sonny Rollins, John Coltrane, and McCoy Tyner. The music had become serious, and it required concentration on the part of listeners. Audiences would sit quietly in rapt attention while the cool sounds of the Modern Jazz Quartet wafted over them.

Dizzy Gillespie (below) introduced new forms of jazz that were inspired by Afro-Cuban rhythms.

Rebels With Paint

What if an artist set out to create art specifically to outrage and shock people? And what if the intended audience not only refused to be offended but took an interest in the new kind of art? This is what happened in the art world during the 1950s.

Painters who, like the Beatniks, rejected conformity and materialism, were determined to rebel against limits on how they could paint. The first step in eliminating boundaries was to do away with the subject—there would be no recognizable image.

Paintings, which tended to be huge, were abstract, and artists such as Jackson Pollock became known as abstract expression-ists. In a sense, abstract expressionist paintings were often about the act of painting itself. Pollock devised a way to drip paint onto huge canvases stretched out on the floor. Others attacked the canvas, lunging with a knife or trowel. Active painters such as these were called Action Painters.

Art lovers at first were mostly baffled by the displays of blobs, drips, and scribbles. But gradually, the public came to accept and value the paintings of the would-be rebels. And within a few years, abstract expressionist paintings were not only hanging in art galleries and museums, but could also be seen decorating the walls of corporate offices.

The Brooklyn Dodgers—"Bums" No Longer

Brooklyn Dodger fans were certainly among the most loyal and devoted fans in the history of baseball. Most likely, the perception of the Dodgers as a perpetual underdog helped stir up the passion of the fans, who affectionately referred to their favorite team as "dem Bums," in the local Brooklyn accent. Time and time again, the Brooklyn Dodgers would come close to winning the World Series. And each time they would lose. The Dodgers faced their rivals, the New York Yankees, in the World Series in 1941, 1947, 1949, 1952, and 1953. Each time, the Dodgers lost, even though they had exceptionally fine ball players such as Jackie Robinson, Gil Hodges, Roy Campanella, and Johnny Podres. "Wait till next year," became the theme song of the Brooklyn Dodgers.

But then, in 1955, "Dem Bums" finally defeated the New York Yankees in the World Series! The Brooklyn Dodgers were "Bums" no longer. Unfortunately, the joy was short-lived. In the 1956 World Series, the Dodgers lost to the New York Yankees once again. Then, in 1958, the Brooklyn Dodgers moved away and became the Los Angeles Dodgers. Some fans never forgave "dem Bums" for leaving Brooklyn.

Roy Campanella (with Yankees catcher Yogi Berra, above) was the first African-American catcher to play in the major leagues, coming to play for the Dodgers in 1948.

Rocky Marciano: Heavyweight Champion

Considered one of the "hardest punchers" in boxing history, Rocky Marciano held the world heavyweight boxing championship title from 1952 to 1956. Born in Massachusetts as Rocco Marchegiano, Marciano won his heavyweight title in September 1952 by defeating Jersey Joe Walcott. Marciano successfully defended his heavyweight title six times. He retired undefeated in 1956, having won all of his forty-nine professional fights.

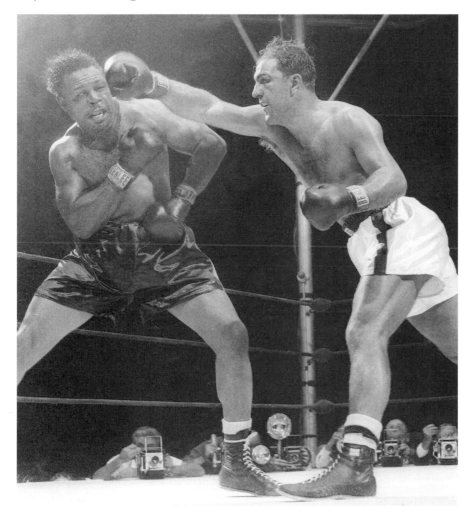

Born in Brockton, Massachusetts, Rocky Marciano (left, at right, fighting Jersey Joe Walcott in 1952) turned professional in 1947. He went on to become one of the most famous boxers of all time.

Ben Hogan: Great American Golfer

In 1953, the Associated Press named golfer Ben Hogan the male athlete of the year. The honor was well earned. Throughout his career, Hogan won more than sixty tournaments. He won the United States Open four times, the Masters twice, the Professional Golfers' Association (PGA) twice, and the British Open once. One of those tournament wins especially showed Hogan's tremendous ability to overcome obstacles. In 1949, Hogan was seriously injured in a car accident. Just seventeen months after the accident, still wearing bandages on his legs, Hogan not only played in the 1950 United States Open, but actually won the tournament!

Ben Hogan (above) was the most dominant golfer of the 1950s.

Althea Gibson: Breaking Barriers in Tennis

For many years, tennis was predominantly a sport for white men, at least professionally. In the 1950s, Althea Gibson changed all that. One of the leading women's amateur players from 1950 to 1958, Gibson became the first well-known African-American tennis player. Among other major victories, Gibson won two consecutive Wimbledon singles titles in 1957 and 1958, as well as the United States Open singles titles in both those years. She was the first African-American player to win these important tournaments.

Born in Silver, South Carolina, in 1927, Althea Gibson spent most of her childhood in New York City. After she began playing amateur tennis in the early 1940s, Gibson made great strides both for women and for African Americans. She ended her tennis career in 1958, then went on to become a professional golfer. Her efforts helped open the world of tennis to future African-American players.

Although the United States and the Soviet Union had been allies during World War II, soon after the war ended, the two nations began to regard each other as a threat. Relations became so strained that a "Cold War" began. Cartoons in America and its non-Communist allies depicted the Soviet menace to freedom around the world.

The Red Scare

On February 9, 1950, Joseph McCarthy, a Republican senator from Wisconsin, announced that he had a list of 205 Communists who worked in the State Department. If this sensational charge were true, then America was in deep trouble. But in speeches over the next few days, McCarthy was vague when reporters asked for details. His list of 205 names shrank to 57, and then to just 4 names. It was also not clear whether the people named were actually Communists, Communist sympathizers, or people who somehow helped the cause of communism. But details did not seem to matter to the senator, or to many of his listeners.

Representing the army in the controversial Army-McCarthy hearings was attorney Joseph Welch, who successfully refuted all of McCarthy's charges. When Welch could listen no longer to McCarthy's cruel treatment of witnesses, he said, "Have you left no sense of decency?" The hearings, which were televised to large audiences, finally gave Americans a chance to see Joseph McCarthy (right) and his ridiculous behavior and unfair tactics firsthand.

And so began McCarthy's four-year campaign of accusations and threats. McCarthy had shrewdly concluded that playing on Americans' fears of communism was a good way to win political power. People from Hollywood, the media, politics, and other walks of life were brought before McCarthy's committee and questioned by McCarthy and his faithful assistants—Roy Cohn and G. David Schine.

Many people lost their jobs as a result of McCarthy's activities. Careers were destroyed and lives were wrecked. McCarthy, in a short time, became one of the most powerful and feared men in America. Few of his fellow politicians were willing to speak against him. They knew that many Americans at the time were genuinely afraid of communism.

Americans stood by while McCarthy continued to harass people. But in the fall of 1953, McCarthy finally bit off more than he could chew. He went after the United States Army, claiming he would expose the Communists lurking there.

The Army-McCarthy hearings in 1954 were televised daily to an audience of 80 million viewers. On television, Americans saw McCarthy's mean-spirited behavior. This was the beginning of the end for McCarthy. Public opinion turned against him. Later that year, the Senate condemned McCarthy for his behavior. McCarthy lost his influence. He died in May 1957 from complications due to alcoholism.

Atomic Spies

When the Soviet Union exploded an atomic bomb in 1949, Americans were shocked. Americans had assumed that the Soviet Union was far behind the United States in science and technology. It seemed that the only way the Soviets could have built a bomb was by stealing secrets from the United States. And the United States government was determined to expose spies who gave away secrets, and put a stop to nuclear espionage.

In 1950, the Federal Bureau of Investigation (FBI) arrested Julius and Ethel Rosenberg. They had been named as members of a spy ring plotting to pass atomic secrets to the Soviets. The couple claimed they were innocent and would give no further information. The Rosenbergs had been active members of the Communist

In light of growing anticommunist hysteria during the Red Scare, it was understandable that some Americans would believe that Soviet spies were at work, giving out vital information about America's nuclear know-how. The Rosenbergs (below) were considered dangerous people who were trying to bring about the downfall of the United States.

party during the 1930s but dropped out in 1943, when their first son was born. Ethel's brother, David Greenglass, had confessed to being part of the spy ring. He claimed that he had handed over secret documents to the Rosenbergs.

On March 29, 1951, a jury convicted the Rosenbergs of espionage. And on April 5, Judge Irving Kaufman sentenced them to die in the electric chair. According to Kaufman, the Rosenbergs' crime was "worse than murder." Recent evidence shows that Julius Rosenberg was indeed guilty of spying. His wife, on the other hand, was not, although she knew of her husband's activities.

Many Americans at the time felt that the Rosenbergs' sentence was too harsh. But many others believed the Rosenbergs had received a fair trial. In any case, the government was determined to make an example of them. On June 19, 1953, the Rosenbergs died in the electric chair.

The Korean War

"We are going to fight!" said President Harry Truman to his daughter, Margaret, on June 25, 1950, on learning that the Communist North Korean Army had just invaded South Korea. Two days later, Truman, with the approval of the United Nations (UN) Security Council, ordered American military forces to help defend the South Koreans against the Communists. America was at war again, just five years after the end of World War II.

By 1950, it seemed to the United States that the Communist Soviet Union and China were bent on world domination. The "free world"—the United States and its allies—would have to preserve its democratic way of life. When World War II ended in 1945, Korea, which had been

President Truman thought it was the United States' duty to force the North Korean troops that had invaded South Korea back to their own side of the 38th parallel. In response to the North Korean invasion, Truman signed an order (above), sending American troops to fight in Korea.

occupied by the Japanese, was divided by an agreement between the United States and the Soviet Union. North Korea became a Communist nation under dictator Kim Il Sung. South Korea was ruled by anticommunist dictator Syngman Rhee.

By 1950, the leaders of North and South Korea began boasting that they would unify all of Korea under their own rule. When the Soviet-supported North Korean Army finally invaded the South, the Cold War reached a boiling point. The North Koreans refused to withdraw. So the United Nations authorized forces, mainly American troops, to push them back.

Once the North Koreans began their invasion, they quickly captured Seoul, the South Korean capital, and pushed deep into the southern part of the country. The situation looked bleak. Then, American General Douglas MacArthur, in charge of the United Nations forces, devised a brilliant but risky

strategy. On September 15, 1950, his troops surprised the North Koreans at Inchon, 150 miles behind enemy lines. The North Korean Army was forced to retreat.

General Douglas MacArthur

The war should have ended once the North Koreans left the South. After all, that had been the goal of the United States and United Nations intervention. But now, President Truman, with the encouragement of General MacArthur, saw an opportunity to invade the North and unite both Koreas under the rule of the South. So the goal was revised.

With the approval of the United Nations, MacArthur's forces pushed northward. MacArthur assured President Truman that there was nothing to worry about—the Chinese

General Douglas MacArthur (with President Truman, above), who had achieved fame as Supreme Allied Commander of the Pacific during World War II, led the UN forces in the Korean War.

would not attack. But suddenly, waves of Chinese troops swept across the border. During the bitterly cold winter of 1950–1951, the American forces suffered high casualties and were driven back to the 38th parallel.

MacArthur came up with another plan. He tried to convince Truman that they could win the war by bombing Chinese air bases in Manchuria. MacArthur would not take no for an answer. The Truman administration thought the most sensible plan was to forget about uniting the two Koreas and to seek a peace agreement that kept the country divided.

When MacArthur heard that Truman was planning to seek a cease-fire, he decided to challenge Truman's strategy. MacArthur spoke out in public, arguing against the president's plans. President Truman, who was MacArthur's Commander in Chief, was furious. Although MacArthur was widely admired by Americans, his conduct was unacceptable. On April 11, 1951, Truman fired MacArthur. The soldier who would not obey orders was relieved of his command.

Eisenhower Becomes President

Peace negotiations in Korea began in July 1951 and continued throughout 1952, but progress was slow. And while the talks went on, fighting continued. Dwight D. Eisenhower, the popular war hero of World War II, was the Republican presidential candidate in

Dwight David Eisenhower (below with his wife, Mamie), the famous general who had led the Allied troops in the D-Day invasion of France, became the thirty-fourth president in 1953.

the 1952 elections. He promised that, if elected, he would promptly end the war in Korea and make sure that Americans continued to enjoy prosperity at home. Americans liked what they heard. And they liked "Ike," as Eisenhower came to be called.

Adlai Stevenson was the Democrats' candidate. But many Americans felt it was time for a change. There had not been a Republican president in office since Herbert Hoover in the early 1930s. So Americans proved how much they liked Ike by electing him president.

Eisenhower kept his promise to end the Korean War. An armistice was signed on July 27, 1953. There were no winners in Korea. It remained a land divided, as it had been before the war began. North and South Korea were in ruins, their economies destroyed, and both sides had suffered hundreds of thousands of casualties. America had also lost some thirty-four thousand soldiers.

Eisenhower proved to be a popular, although somewhat dull, president. His administration tended to favor the interests of big business. However, Eisenhower was involved in a large expansion of the Social Security system. He worked toward passage of the first civil rights act (1957) since Reconstruction ended in 1877. He also helped provide the first major federal funding for education and established the Department of Health, Education, and Welfare (HEW) as a Cabinet position in 1953. In 1956, voters still liked Ike. They re-elected him to four more years in the White House.

At the end of Eisenhower's second four-year presidential term, he offered a warning to the American people. During his years as president, the old general had come to realize that a combination of powerful interests—the military establishment

and the huge arms industry, supported by politicians, America's largest corporations, and defense research scholars—threatened to tie the nation's economic health to enormous defense budgets as far ahead as the eye could see. During his farewell to the nation just three days before leaving office, Eisenhower warned that "We must guard against the acquisition of unwarranted influence . . . by the military-industrial complex. The potential for the disastrous rise of misplaced power exists and will persist."

The Bracero Program

During World War II, many American farms, as well as certain industries such as railroads and trucking, relied on workers from Mexico to alleviate the labor shortage in the United States. In the past, the Mexicans had often been treated badly. Forced to labor under terrible working conditions, they had to live in housing that often consisted of nothing more than a chicken coop, and often had nothing better to eat than leftover scraps of food. Unscrupulous employers sometimes did not even pay their Mexican workers.

In response to the labor shortage, the U.S. government sought to encourage Mexicans to become temporary workers in this country. The government created the bracero program to enable American employers to recruit Mexicans. The word *bracero* (from *brazo*, or "arm" in Spanish) means someone who works with his arms, a hired hand. The program was supposed to guarantee a minimum wage, encourage fair labor practices, and protect the health and well-being of the Mexican workers. But the abuse of Mexican workers continued.

Nevertheless, during the first bracero program, from 1942 to 1947, about 250,000 Mexicans were hired to work seasonally in the United States. During the second bracero program, from 1948 to 1964, more than 4.5 million Mexicans came to work in the United States. At the height of the program, in 1956, some 445,000 Mexicans worked in agriculture in the United States.

Fighting for Civil Rights

For years since the end of the Civil War, African Americans, especially in the South, had to use separate facilities from white Americans—everything from separate rest rooms to separate drinking fountains. Racist whites, who refused to grant blacks the equal rights they had won after the Civil War, referred to this system as "separate but equal."

On May 17, 1954, the United States Supreme Court, in *Brown* v. *Board of Education of Topeka, Kansas*, finally ruled that separate facilities, in regard to education, were inherently unequal. At the time, 40 percent of American public schools were still segregated, or separated by race. The Supreme Court ordered them to be desegregated.

Among the tactics used by racist whites to "keep blacks in their place" was the Jim Crow system. Jim Crow, or segregation, laws were put in place throughout the South. The laws created separate facilities, such as drinking fountains (above) for African Americans.

Even so, people's prejudices did not vanish overnight. When African-American students tried to enter what had been all-white schools, they faced the bitter defiance of many Southern whites. For several years, there was very little progress in desegregating schools. Then, in 1957, African Americans in Little Rock, Arkansas, won a court order allowing nine African-American students to enter Little Rock's Central High School. Arkansas Governor Orval Faubus, who opposed school integration, ordered the Arkansas National Guard to block the entrance to the school. For the next three weeks, photos of armed troops preventing the nine students from entering the school appeared in newspapers all across the country. On September 24, 1957, President Eisenhower sent a

Rosa Parks arrives at court in Montgomery, Alabama, to be arraigned in the racial bus boycott in February 1956. Parks was fined for refusing to give up her seat at the front of a bus.

thousand army troops to Little Rock. On September 25, they made sure the African-American students were allowed into the school.

Rosa Parks and the Montgomery Bus Boycott

Meanwhile, civil rights progress was being made in other areas. On December 1, 1955, Rosa Parks, an African-American seamstress, was riding on a bus in Montgomery, Alabama.

The United States Supreme Court knew the Brown case would be a landmark decision that would affect race relations for years to come. Its members wanted the decision to be unanimous. Arguing the case before the Supreme Court was Thurgood Marshall, who would later become the first African-American Supreme Court justice.

When the bus driver ordered her to give up her seat to a white man, she refused, thereby breaking the law. She was arrested, put on trial, convicted, and fined. Inspired by Rosa Parks's courageous act, Dr. Martin Luther King, Jr., and other black civil rights leaders organized a peaceful boycott of Montgomery's bus system. The boycott lasted until December 20, 1956, when the United States Supreme Court ruled that Alabama's bus segregation laws were unconstitutional.

A New Leader for the Soviet Union

Joseph Stalin, the dictator who had ruled the Soviet Union since 1929, died in 1953. Although he had used secret police to terrorize the population and was responsible for the deaths of millions of Soviet citizens, many Soviets mourned his passing.

The new Soviet leader, Nikita Khrushchev, was determined to improve the lives of the Soviet people. After denouncing Stalin's misdeeds in a speech, Khrushchev made it clear that he intended to make reforms. He was in favor of easing the government's strict control of every aspect of life and the official censorship of the arts and media. Under Khrushchev, people began to enjoy a greater degree of freedom to express their views. But while a new day seemed to be dawning at home, the Soviet government maintained its tight grip over the other Communist nations of Eastern Europe.

The Failed Hungarian Revolution

In October 1956, the Hungarian people rose up against the Soviet-backed government in their country. The rebellion became a mass movement, and Hungarian leader Imre Nagy

Nikita Khrushchev (at far left) became leader of the Soviet Union in 1956. He firmly believed that the Soviet system was the best form of government. In July 1959, the city of Moscow held an exhibition at which several displays showed typical life in the United States, including fancy kitchen appliances and televisions. Vice President Richard Nixon attended the exhibition and got into an angry debate with Khrushchev over which system— capitalism or communism— was better. Khrushchev swore that his Communist system would survive long after the fall of capitalism.

(pronounced "Nahj") spoke out about breaking free of the Soviet Union's control. Some Hungarians took the occasion to seek revenge against Soviet secret police, who had killed many Hungarians in the past. Dozens of secret police were lynched. Of course, the Soviet Union was not about to tolerate such a revolt. For several days, Hungarians celebrated their new freedom. The celebration did not last long, however. Soviet troops and tanks soon rolled into Hungary. Many Hungarian freedom fighters tried to resist the invaders. They appealed to the United States for help. But no help came, because the Eisenhower administration did not want to risk a confrontation with the Soviet Union. In the next few days, more than twenty thousand Hungarian citizens were killed. And Imre Nagy was arrested and executed by the Soviets.

Revolution in Cuba: The Rise of Fidel Castro

Fidel Castro (below) established himself as the dictator of Cuba. After taking over American property in the island nation, Castro continued to pose a threat as an ally of the Communist Soviet Union.

Since 1956, a revolution had been occurring only ninety miles away from Key West, Florida, in the Caribbean nation of Cuba. The rebels, under the command of Fidel Castro, were fighting to overthrow the brutal and corrupt dictatorship of Fulgencio Batista. Cuba was wealthy, but the distribution of wealth was very unequal. A small group of families controlled most of the wealth of the island. The rest of the population was very poor. Batista often jailed, tortured, and murdered his political opponents. Most Cubans hated him. Castro, on the other hand, attracted followers and even had admirers in the United States. By the late 1950s, Castro and his guerrilla fighters were gaining the upper hand against Batista's troops. Finally, in January 1959, Batista fled the island. Castro and his troops entered Havana in triumph.

Once in power, Castro instituted reforms to improve the lives of the poorest Cubans. In the process, he seized private companies, turning them into state-run businesses. The United States government was not pleased. Relations between the two countries deteriorated. Ultimately, Castro would embrace communism, turning to the Soviet Union for economic assistance. The United States would have to learn to deal with having a Communist nation as a close neighbor.

The Dawn of the Computer Age

When Remington Rand introduced its UNIVAC computer in 1951, people were amazed at how "small" it was. It was fourteen by seven by nine feet, about the size of a small bedroom! Today, this seems enormous. But UNIVAC was only about one tenth of the size of earlier computers.

Throughout the 1950s, computers became smaller, faster, and more powerful machines. Many businesses and academic institutions could finally afford them. Transistors replaced vacuum tubes, making the smaller machines possible. The silicon microchip, a small wafer of silicon, was developed in 1958–1959. Jack Kilby at Texas Instruments placed electronic circuits onto microchips. Robert Noyce at Fairchild Semiconductor invented a way to connect microchip circuits. Continual advances in miniaturization in the decades to come would eventually lead to today's hand-held computers that have greater capabilities than the room-sized UNIVAC of the 1950s.

John William Mauchley (left) and John Presper Eckert, Jr. (right), created UNIVAC, or Universal Automatic Computer. The United States Census Bureau bought the first UNIVAC to help tabulate the results of its 1950 population count.

Software programs were another major innovation. One of the earliest programming languages was FORTRAN, which was used for science and mathematics. Then came COBOL, or Common Business Oriented Language, which was used for business. This was the start of what is known today as the Information Age.

Sputnik 1 Delivers a Wake-up Call

On October 4, 1957, the Soviet Union launched *Sputnik 1*, the world's first man-made satellite, into orbit around the earth. Many Americans reacted with shock, outrage, and fear at this demonstration of Soviet superiority in space. Secretary of Defense Charles Wilson tried to calm fears by saying *Sputnik* was nothing more than a "neat scientific trick." President Eisenhower said there was nothing to worry about "as far as security is concerned." Most Americans, of course, disagreed. The United States was involved in a nuclear arms race with the Soviet Union. It now appeared likely that America's rival would soon be able to launch nuclear missiles at the United States from space. Americans were amazed that their country could have fallen so far behind the Soviet Union in rocket technology. Suddenly, government money began to pour into space research.

When the United States successfully launched its first satellite, *Explorer 1*, into orbit on January 31, 1958, Soviet leader Nikita Khrushchev had a good laugh. He pointed out that the American satellite weighed only thirty pounds, whereas the

Sputnik (below), launched in 1957, circled Earth at eighteen thousand miles an hour, completing its orbit once every ninety-six minutes. Although it caused a scare among many Americans who feared its potential destructive power, *Sputnik* itself was destroyed when it fell to Earth in January 1958.

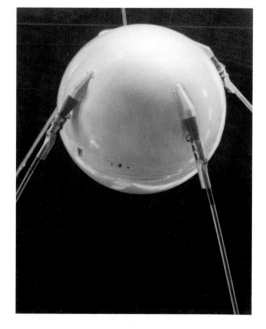

Soviets were launching satellites that weighed more than a thousand pounds. He referred to *Explorer 1* as a "little grapefruit." But America would ultimately have the last laugh when the Apollo astronauts won the space race by walking on the surface of the moon a decade later.

Determining the Structure of DNA

Scientists were also involved in work outside the space race. They were making great progress in learning how the human body works. Genes within the DNA (deoxyribonucleic acid) in the nucleus of each of our cells carry the code for manufacturing the various proteins that allow the cells to function. Until the 1950s, very little was known about the structure of DNA and how genes function.

In the early 1950s, Rosalind Franklin used an X-ray photographic technique to determine that DNA is helical, or spiral, in form. Then, in 1953, American biologist James Watson worked with English biophysicist Francis Crick to discover that DNA is formed by two helixes wound around each other. They then found that the double helix could unwind to allow the structure to duplicate itself exactly. These discoveries would lead to breakthroughs in the study of the genetic code on which all life is based, and an understanding of which genes are responsible for certain characteristics in human beings.

Swiss biochemist Friedrich Miescher had discovered DNA in 1868, but it was not until the 1950s that scientists learned about its structure or how it works. Watson and Crick were the first to describe DNA as a double helix, or a structure that resembles a twisting ladder (left). In 1957, an American scientist named Arthur Kornberg made DNA in a test tube. The work of these scientists led to the complex research now being done in biogenetics.

The Man Who Conquered Polio

Epidemics of polio, often referred to as "infantile paralysis," had long occurred in many parts of the world, including the United States, Europe, and Asia. A particularly severe outbreak of the disease had begun in the United States in 1942 and continued into the 1950s. In 1950 alone there were some thirty-three thousand reported cases.

Jonas Salk, an American research scientist, had begun working in 1947 to find a way to prevent the crippling disease. After several years of painstaking work in his laboratory, Salk found that, by injecting a killed polio virus into a person, the

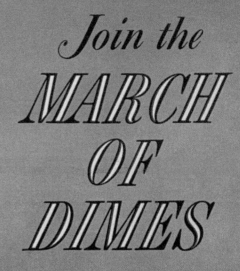

"*Look!* I can walk again"

Join the
MARCH
OF
DIMES

FIGHT
INFANTILE
PARALYSIS

THE NATIONAL FOUNDATION FOR INFANTILE PARALYSIS

FRANKLIN D. ROOSEVELT, FOUNDER

body could build up an immunity to stronger forms of the virus. He developed a polio vaccine and proved it was safe by testing it on himself, his wife, and his children.

In 1954, more than 1.8 million schoolchildren were injected with the vaccine. In 1955, the vaccine was declared safe and effective in preventing polio. A serious disease had been conquered by a man of science.

For decades, polio was a terrible threat to people all over the world. Organizations like the March of Dimes (opposite) supported the development of Dr. Jonas Salk's vaccine in 1955. On April 22, 1955, Salk received a citation from President Eisenhower and a congressional gold medal for "great achievement in the field of medicine" (left).

In the 1950s, Americans were involved in combat overseas once again, as they tried to contain communism. Below, U.S. Marines land on a ridge in Korea via helicopter in September 1951.

An Amazing Decade

The 1950s were a time of great prosperity for many Americans, as well as a period of contrast and change. Middle-class families were doing well in the years after World War II. Millions of children were being born, and families who could afford it were fulfilling dreams of home ownership in the suburbs. Television portrayed middle-class life as an ideal. Americans huddled together to watch their favorite television stars live wonderful lives in an idealized, fictitious suburban world.

At the same time, Americans were often huddling not around the television, but in fear. The tense years of the Cold War, the arms race, and Senator McCarthy's hunt for Communists caused people to fear a nuclear war could occur at any time. Even children, who took part in duck-and-cover drills and watched their families build fallout shelters, felt this overwhelming apprehension. Others had different fears. African Americans feared racist violence as they struggled to win the civil rights denied them for so long.

The 1950s were marked by all of these ups and downs. From the terror caused by *Sputnik* to the birth of rock 'n' roll, from the war in Korea to the poodle skirt, the 1950s were truly a unique and amazing decade.

Timeline

1950 **Christian Dior**'s "New Look" is the height of fashion; **Ben Hogan** wins the United States Open golf tournament; **Joseph McCarthy** announces that he has a list of Communists working in the State Department, beginning the McCarthy Red Scare; **Ethel** and **Julius Rosenberg** are arrested for espionage; North Korea invades South Korea, beginning the Korean War.

1951 **J. D. Salinger** publishes *The Catcher in the Rye*; The **Rosenbergs** are convicted of espionage; President **Harry Truman** fires General **Douglas MacArthur**; UNIVAC computer is introduced.

1952 **Rocky Marciano** first wins world heavyweight title; **Dwight D. Eisenhower** is elected president on the Republican ticket.

1953 Movies *War of the Worlds*, *House of Wax*, and *It Came from Outer Space* released; **Marilyn Monroe** stars in *Gentlemen Prefer Blondes* and *How to Marry a Millionaire*; **Ben Hogan** becomes Associated Press Male Athlete of the Year; The **Rosenbergs** die in the electric chair; Armistice signed in the Korean War; Eisenhower administration establishes Department of Health, Education, and Welfare; Soviet leader **Joseph Stalin** dies; Scientists **James Watson** and **Francis Crick** discover the structure and function of DNA.

1954 **Marlon Brando** stars in *The Wild One*; *Creature from the Black Lagoon* released; Army-McCarthy hearings take place, with the help of McCarthy aide **Roy Cohn**; United States Supreme Court hands down its *Brown* v. *Board of Education* decision.

1955 *Rebel Without a Cause* opens in theaters; *The Blackboard Jungle* draws attention to gang-related violence in New York City; **Brooklyn**

Dodgers defeat the **New York Yankees** in the World Series; **Rosa Parks** inspires African-American leaders, including **Martin Luther King**, to start the Montgomery Bus Boycott; **Jonas Salk**'s polio vaccine is declared safe and effective.

1956 Congress passes the National Defense Highway Act to build more highways for defense and recreational driving; Film *Invasion of the Body Snatchers* becomes a hit; *The Ten Commandments* opens in theaters; **Rocky Marciano** retires from professional boxing; **Dwight Eisenhower** is re-elected president; United States Supreme Court declares bus segregation laws in Montgomery, Alabama, unconstitutional; **Nikita Khrushchev** becomes leader of Soviet Union; Hungary attempts to revolt against Soviet control.

1957 **Jack Kerouac** publishes *On the Road*; **Brooklyn Dodgers** move at the end of the baseball season to become the Los Angeles Dodgers; **Althea Gibson** becomes the first black person to win Wimbledon and the United States Open singles tennis titles; Senator **Joseph McCarthy** dies; First civil rights act since Reconstruction is passed; **President Eisenhower** sends troops to help integrate Little Rock's Central High School; Soviet Union launches *Sputnik 1*.

1958 **Althea Gibson**, for the second consecutive year, wins Wimbledon and United States Open singles titles; United States launches *Explorer 1*; The Hula Hoop is introduced.

1959 Film *Ben-Hur* opens in theaters; **Marilyn Monroe** appears in *Some Like It Hot*; **Fidel Castro** succeeds in ousting Cuban dictator **Fulgencio Batista** and becomes the dictator of Cuba.

Further Reading

Books

The American Dream: The 50s. Alexandria, Va.: Time-Life Books, 1998.

Evans, Harold. *The American Century*. New York: Alfred A. Knopf, 1998.

Jennings, Peter, and Todd Brewster. *The Century*. New York: Doubleday, 1998.

Junior Chronicle of the 20th Century. New York: DK Publishing, 1997.

Kallen, Stuart A. *The 1950s*. San Diego, Calif.: Greenhaven Press, 1998.

Zeinert, Karen. *McCarthy and the Fear of Communism in American History*. Springfield, N.J.: Enslow Publishers, Inc., 1998.

Internet Addresses

Cold War Museum
http://www.coldwar.org/

Korean War Project
http://www.koreanwar.org/

Dwight D. Eisenhower
http://www.whitehouse.gov/history/presidents/de34.html

The Fifties Index
http://www.fiftiesweb.com/

Index

A

abstract expressionists, 25–26
Action Painters. *See* abstract expressionists.
African Americans, 30, 31, 44–48, 59
air-raid drills, 13–14
American Bandstand, 24
Army-McCarthy hearings, 34, 35
atomic bomb, 5, 13–15, 35, 36, 59

B

baby boom, 24, 59
Ball, Lucille, 21, 22
Batista, Fulgencio, 50
Beatnik, 10–11, 25
Ben-Hur, 19
Berle, Milton, 22
Berry, Chuck, 23, 24
Blackboard Jungle, The, 18
bracero program, 44
Brando, Marlon, 16, 18
Brooklyn Dodgers, 27–28
Brown v. *Board of Education of Topeka, Kansas*, 45

C

Campanella, Roy, 27–28
Castro, Fidel, 50
Catcher in the Rye, The, 17
China, 36
CinemaScope, 19
civil rights movement, 44–48, 59
Clark, Dick, 24
Cohn, Roy, 34
Cold War, 5, 13, 32, 38, 59
communism, 5, 32–38, 48, 50, 59
credit cards, 8
Crick, Francis, 55
Cuban Revolution, 50

D

Dean, James, 17
deoxyribonucleic acid (DNA), 54–55
Dior, Christian, 13

E

Eisenhower, Dwight D., 40–43, 45, 49, 53
Explorer 1, 53–54

F

fallout shelters, 5, 15, 59
fashion, 10–13, 59
Faubus, Orval, 45
Federal Bureau of Investigation (FBI), 35
Franklin, Rosalind, 55
Frisbee, 15

G

Gibson, Althea, 30, 31
Gillespie, Dizzy, 25
Ginsberg, Allen, 10
Gleason, Jackie, 22
Great Depression, 7
Greenglass, David, 36

H

Hodges, Gil, 27
Hogan, Ben, 30
Hula-Hoop, 15
Hungarian Revolution, 48–50

J

jazz, 24–25

K

Kerouac, Jack, 10–11
Khrushchev, Nikita, 48, 53
King, Martin Luther, Jr., 48
Korean War, 5, 36–40, 42, 59

L

Little Rock, Arkansas, school desegregation, 45–46

M

MacArthur, Douglas, 39–40
Marciano, Rocky, 29
McCarthy, Joseph, 5, 33–35, 59
Monroe, Marilyn, 22–23
Montgomery, Alabama, bus boycott, 48

N

Nagy, Imre, 48–50
National Defense Highway Act, 9
New York Yankees, 27–28

O

On the Road, 11

P

Parks, Rosa, 46, 48
Podres, Johnny, 27

polio vaccine, 57
Pollock, Jackson, 25–26
Presley, Elvis, 23–24

R

Rebel Without a Cause, 17
Rhee, Syngman, 38
Robinson, Jackie, 27
rock 'n' roll, 23–24
Rosenberg, Ethel, 35–36
Rosenberg, Julius, 35–36

S

Salinger, J. D., 17
Salk, Jonas, 55, 57
Schine, G. David, 34
science fiction, 18–19
Silly Putty, 15
Slinky, 15
Soviet Union, 5, 13, 35, 36, 38, 48–50, 53–54
Sputnik 1, 53, 59
Stalin, Joseph, 48
Stevenson, Adlai, 42

suburbs, 5, 9–10, 59
Sung, Kim Il, 38

T

television, 5, 7, 20–22, 59
Ten Commandments, The, 19
3-D films, 19–20
Truman, Harry, 36, 37, 39, 40

U

United Nations, 36, 38, 39
United States Supreme Court, 45, 47
UNIVAC, 51, 52

W

Walcott, Jersey Joe, 29
Watson, James, 55
Westerns, 20
Wild One, The, 18
Wilson, Charles, 53
working women, 11, 13
World War II, 5, 7, 24, 36, 40, 59